water

EXPERIMENTS TO UNDERSTAND IT

by Boris Arnov
Illustrated by Giulio Maestro

Lothrop, Lee & Shepard Books
New York

water
EXPERIMENTS TO UNDERSTAND IT

In clear memory of my mother;
this book is for you.

3   4   5   6   7   8   9   10

Library of Congress Cataloging in Publication Data

Arnov, Boris.
  Water: experiments to understand it.

  SUMMARY: Properties of water are demonstrated through simple experiments.
  1. Water-Experiments—Juvenile literature. [1. Water—Experiments.   2. Experiments] I. Maestro, Giulio.   II. Title.
QC145.2.A76   546'.22   79-24297
ISBN 0-688-41927-5   ISBN 0-688-51927-X lib. bdg.

Contents

A WORD TO THE READER:

This book contains experiments that are designed to help you increase your understanding of water, that remarkable substance too many of us take for granted. You will find that the materials for each experiment are easy to find, and you should have no difficulty following the instructions and arriving at the conclusions stated. If things do not always turn out the way they were supposed to, try again. A large part of success in experimenting is having good techniques, and this will come with practice.

Getting to know and understand more about anything usually leads to a greater appreciation of it. If, through these experiments, this happens to you and you do come to value water more than ever before, then perhaps you will help to conserve this material without which life would be impossible.

1

Density

Water's weight or density changes, depending upon its temperature or the amount of dissolved minerals it contains.

THE EXPERIMENTS

1

Materials: Hot and cold water, clear glass or plastic containers, food coloring, and a medicine dropper or straw.

Procedure:
1. Half fill the glass or plastic container with cold water.
2. Half fill another container with hot water and add a few drops of food coloring.
3. Carefully add the colored hot water to the cold water. This can be done by pouring slowly, by using a medicine

dropper, or by using a straw. Immerse the straw in the colored water, clamp your finger tightly across the top hole, and lift the water column in the straw from one container to the other. Remove your finger to release the water.

4. Observe what happens.

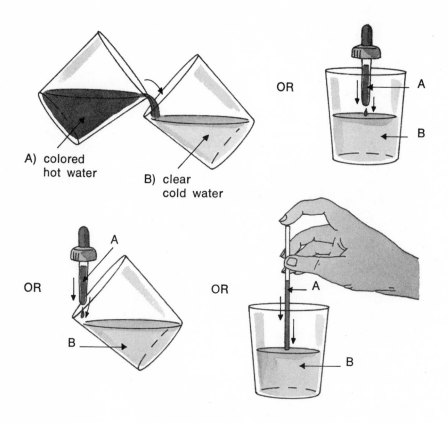

A) colored hot water

B) clear cold water

OR

OR

OR

A

B

Conclusion: Note how the colored water remains on top of the clear water, thus proving that hot water is lighter or less dense than cool water.

Materials: Water, containers, and salt. (Table salt has an additive that clouds the water, so pickling salt or the kosher variety is preferred.)

Procedure:
1. Half fill a container with tap water.
2. Stir in and dissolve several tablespoons of salt.
3. Half fill a container with tap water and add a few drops of food coloring.
4. As you did in Experiment 1, carefully add the colored water to the clear.
5. Observe what happens.

Conclusion: Note how the colored water remains on top of the clear water, thus proving that it is less dense or lighter than salt water.

3

Materials: The same as the preceding experiments.

Procedure:
1. Reverse the procedure in Experiment 1 by adding cold water to hot and note how, if carefully done, the cold water sinks to form a layer beneath the hot.

Conclusion: Cold water, being heavier and therefore denser than hot, sinks beneath it.

2. Reverse the procedure in Experiment 2 by adding salt

water to fresh. If carefully done, the salt water will sink and form a layer beneath the fresh.

Conclusion: Salt water, being heavier and therefore denser, sinks in fresh water.

THE RELEVANCE

Consider a lake in a part of the world where it is cold enough to freeze during the winter. As cold autumn winds blow upon the surface, water is cooled and, as you know from the experiments you performed, it becomes heavier or denser than deeper water which has been insulated from the cold winds above. The surface water, therefore, sinks in the lake.

Just as you cannot fill a one-quart container with two quarts of liquid, surface water cannot sink unless space is made for it to do so. What happens is similar to what you observed when cold water was added to hot: hot water is displaced and forms a layer above the colder, heavier water, thus making space for it to sink. In a lake, warm subsurface water rises to the top.

But this process does not stop there, for cold winds continue to blow on the lake's surface and the same phenomenon as before occurs: as surface water cools and becomes denser it sinks to the bottom, causing more water displacement. As a matter of fact, this occurs so continuously that a sort of up-to-down and down-to-up circulation takes place in the lake as all its water changes place. In this way the entire lake basin gets a complete flushing, the importance of which will be taken up in Chapter 3.

As you discovered in the experiment, fresh water actually floats on salt water as when a river flows into the sea. This

can often be observed at an inlet where fresh and salt water meet. As the fresh water flows out to sea, it blankets the salt water and continues to do so for miles around until winds and strong ocean currents force the two to mix.

Sometimes, however, if fresh water is very cold it actually may be denser than warm salt water. Icebergs that flow down the Davis Strait between Labrador and Newfoundland meet the warm waters of the Atlantic Ocean's Gulf Stream. As melting occurs, very cold fresh water sinks beneath ocean water and gradually spreads over the sea floor until it warms and mixes.

2

Water Expands and Contracts

THE IDEA

Most substances expand when heated and contract when cooled. Water obeys this rule only to a certain point. At 4 degrees Celsius or 39 degrees Fahrenheit, water expands instead of continuing to contract and does so until it freezes, at 0 degrees C. or 32 degrees F. Ice, therefore, floats, as it is lighter than water.

THE EXPERIMENTS

1

Materials: Copper wire, weight (such as a fishing lead), string, two rigid supports for attaching the wire, and a source of heat such as a candle.

Procedure:

1. Attach a piece of copper wire about 3 feet long to two sup-

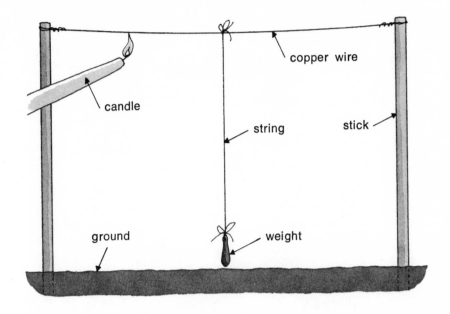

Labels in figure: candle, copper wire, string, stick, ground, weight

ports. This could be two sticks pushed into the ground or the backs of two heavy chairs.

2. Attach the lead with string to the middle of the stretched wire. This should be done so that the weight nearly touches the floor or some object you place beneath it.
3. Using the candle, heat the wire by passing the flame over as much of it as you can.
4. Observe whether the lead weight changes position or not.

Conclusion: Because the heat caused the wire to expand, it lengthened and allowed the weight to touch the floor. Note that as the wire cools, the weight lifts away from the floor, demonstrating that the wire has contracted.

2

Materials: Measuring cup, pot or pan, and the kitchen range.

Procedure:
1. Pour cold water into the measuring cup and record the exact level it reaches.
2. Pour this water into a pan or pot and heat to just below the boiling point.
3. Pour back into the measuring cup and note where the level now is.

Conclusion: Upon being heated, water expands and occupies more space than it did when cool.

3

Materials: Plastic container with a tight-fitting lid, water, and the freezing compartment of a refrigerator.

Procedure:
1. Fill the plastic container with so much water that some flows over when you put the lid on the container.
2. Place the container in the freezer compartment of a refrigerator and after the water has frozen, note its condition.

Conclusion: The fact that the ice has either pushed up the lid or broken the container indicates that upon freezing, water expands.

THE RELEVANCE

Think for a moment what would happen if water acted like other substances. As cold winter temperatures continued to fall, eventually to freeze the surface water of a pond or a lake, the ice, if it were like other materials, would be at its densest and therefore would sink to the bottom. As the temperature at the surface remained cold, more ice would form and sink, eventually freezing the lake from the bottom up. Most of the animals and plants could not stand such severe conditions and would die.

But from what you discovered, that water expands upon freezing, lakes do not freeze from the bottom up. Instead, frozen surface water floats like an ice cube in a glass of water. Unless it is unusually cold or it is a very small pond, there remains throughout the winter a layer of water beneath the ice, and the plants and animals, though restricted in their activities, at least are able to survive until spring when the ice thaws.

3

Overturn

THE IDEA

Circulation of water in some lakes is accomplished by overturn, a phenomenon that occurs when heavy surface water sinks to displace sediment-containing bottom water, which rises to the surface.

THE EXPERIMENT

Materials: Cold water, a measuring cup, sediment collected from a lake bottom or flour used for baking, and a glass or plastic container (the taller, the better).

Procedure:
1. Fill the container with water to about two inches from its top.
2. Add sediment or flour and allow time for it to settle, perhaps a day or two.

3. Carefully add about two ounces of ice water by pouring it slowly against the inside of the container.
4. Observe what happens.

cold water

sediment

Conclusion: As the ice water sank to the bottom it displaced the sediment-containing bottom water, which then rose to the top.

During the times of the year when there is little or no water circulation, lake bottoms accumulate sediment composed of dead animal and plant life that has not been eaten by living organisms. Added to the sediment is other matter such as mineral-laden soil washed from the shore by waves and rain. Were it not for circulation of the water, these materials, important primarily as fertilizing agents to all plant life in the lake, would remain at the bottom and never mix with the rest of the lake's layers. Also, oxygen-laden surface waters would never sink to become available to deeper life forms that need this gas to live (see Chapter 5).

This is what happens in deep lakes in warm climates: surface water never cools to the point that it is heavier than deeper water; therefore, it never sinks. The result is that all solid matter in the lake sinks to the bottom and never rises back to the surface. Oxygen never travels deep and so such a lake is devoid of life in its deeper regions. Only some bacteria can live in these regions of such a lake.

Overturns, with the occasional help of wind and other forces, completely circulate the waters of deep lakes in temperate climates and thereby make oxygen and minerals available to life in all layers of water. During the late fall, declining air temperature gradually cools surface water which, as you learned in Chapter 1, sinks and creates circulation. During the spring the ice layer melts and when the surface water reaches its densest state, at about 4 degrees Celsius or 39 degrees Fahrenheit, it sinks and once again creates circulation. Without fall and spring overturns, our lakes would never abound with the plant and animal life characteristic of them.

4

Nutrients

THE IDEA

Minerals dissolved in water, essential chemicals for all life, enter the tissues of plants by passing through microscopic pores in the plant body.

THE EXPERIMENTS

1

Materials: Lake or ocean water, a pan or a large, shallow dish, and a heat source such as the kitchen range.

Procedure:
1. Collect about one quart of water from a lake or the ocean.
2. Pour the water into the shallow dish or pan and allow it to evaporate. As this process might take many days, you can gently heat the water in the pan until most of it is gone.

Then allow the remainder to evaporate in the same pan.
3. Observe what remains in the dish after the water is gone.

Conclusion: The salty material left after evaporation is the dissolved minerals that water contains.

2

Materials: Thin plastic wrap, flour or cornstarch, tincture of iodine, a glass or plastic container, and water.

Procedure:
1. Nearly fill the glass or plastic container with water and stir into it a teaspoon of flour or cornstarch.

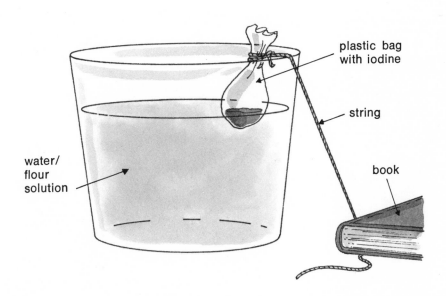

plastic bag
with iodine

string

water/
flour
solution

book

2. Make a small bag of the thin plastic wrap and put into it about a teaspoon of the tincture of iodine. Tie the top tightly so that the iodine solution will not spill.
3. Place the plastic bag in the flour solution. Suspend so that it is immersed a half inch or so. Keep it in place by taping the end of the string to the outside of the container or, if long enough, place a weight such as a book on it.
4. Observe for a day or two.

Conclusion: Iodine passes through microscopic pores in the plastic wrap and reacts with the starch, turning it blue or blue-black.

Overturn, as explained in Chapter 3, distributes throughout a body of water all the sediment and dissolved minerals that accumulate on the bottom. The minerals are brought to the plant-growing levels of the lake or the ocean, the region light can penetrate. Once these minerals are taken in by the aquatic plants, they become available to the tiny animal life that depends upon plants for food.

Larger creatures such as fish get the minerals by eating the smaller animals. In this way, minerals travel through the bodies of all the organisms in a body of water. When the plant and animal life dies and sinks to the bottom, microscopic bacteria reduce this material to a chemical state. The cycle is then complete and the accumulated bottom material has only to wait for another overturn to mix into the waters again.

5

Oxygen

In any body of water—a lake or an aquarium—the greatest concentration of oxygen is at the surface, its origin being the air above. In addition to dispersing minerals throughout a lake, overturn brings oxygen down deep to animal life that must have this gas to live.

THE EXPERIMENT

Materials: Salt (preferably the pickling or kosher variety), water, a one-quart (or slightly more) glass or clear plastic wide-mouth container, red and blue food coloring, a baster, a measuring cup, a medicine dropper, an ice cube tray, and a freezer.

Procedure:
1. The night before you perform this experiment, make blue

ice cubes by freezing water colored deep blue with the food coloring.

2. Place 3 cups of clear water into the quart container.

baster

red salty water

salt-water solution

red salty water

blue ice cubes

red salty water

3. Dissolve 1 tablespoon salt in 2 cups of water.
4. Add red food coloring to the 2 cups of salt water until it is deeply colored.
5. Using the baster, carefully transfer the red salt water to the bottom of the quart container. If done properly it should stay in a layer beneath the clear fresh water. Transfer enough red salt water so that the layer is about one-half inch thick.
6. Carefully place as many blue ice cubes as you can in the quart container. The surface area should be packed with so many ice cubes that any more would force the ice mass lower into the container.
7. Observe what happens over the next several minutes.

Conclusion: As the surface water cools from the ice and becomes heavier than the water beneath it, it sinks, carrying with it the blue color which represents oxygen. In this manner you will observe the blue going all the way to the bottom, where it may not mix with but only rest on the top of the red layer. To mix it with the red layer in the container, using the baster withdraw about one-quarter cup of cold blue water from the surface. Dissolve in this water as much salt as you can. Using the baster again, add some of this cold, salty blue water to the quart container and observe how it immediately sinks to the bottom to disrupt and disperse the red layer. This demonstrates how circulation in a lake can mix water layers together.

THE RELEVANCE

Animals, whether land or water dwellers, need oxygen for respiration. Aquatic animals usually get oxygen directly from the water by means of gills—delicate filaments containing a blood vessel that absorbs gaseous oxygen from the water and transports it to the other blood vessels, and thus to all parts of the animal's system.

Although water plants, like those on land, do produce oxy-

gen in the process of photosynthesis, most of the oxygen in water comes directly from the air above. Consequently, the upper layers of any body of water will always contain more oxygen than the lower strata. Bottom- or deep-dwelling animals do not usually leave the depths to which they are accustomed in order to swim to the surface for oxygen. Rather, some of this gas does travel down, by slow diffusion and by wave and wind action. In contrast, overturn, by completely mixing the water, brings abundant oxygen to all parts of a body of water.

6

Evaporation and Condensation

Heat changes water from its liquid state to a gas, or water vapor, a process called evaporation. Cooling changes water vapor back to its liquid state, a process called condensation.

THE EXPERIMENT

Materials: A teakettle, about 18 inches of tubing of a size to place over the kettle spout (it can be of any material and can even be made of rolled foil), a clear glass bottle with a narrow neck, ice, a pan large enough to contain both bottle and ice, water, and a heat source.

Procedure:
1. Place about a pint of water in the teakettle and attach the tubing to the spout, as airtight as possible. The other end of the tube should be placed in the empty bottle. Place the

bottle in a pan and pack ice around the base of the bottle.
2. Boil the water in the teakettle until you see a few drops of water collecting inside the bottle.

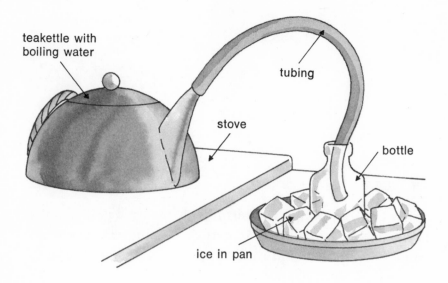

teakettle with
boiling water

tubing

stove

bottle

ice in pan

Conclusion: The energy from heat speeds up water molecules and some move so rapidly that they evaporate or escape into the air as gas or water vapor. As more rise, they push into the tubing and pass through it to enter the bottle, which has been cooled by the ice. At that stage the cold slows down the gaseous water molecules and they come together or condense, once again returning to the liquid state.

On earth there is a natural circulation of water from oceans, lakes, and rivers by evaporation into the air. Then, condensation occurs to produce rain falling to the soil, running off to rivers, lakes, and then to the ocean once again. (Though the ocean is salty and stream water contains many minerals, as you learned in Chapter 4, in evaporation only pure water becomes a gas and substances dissolved in it are left behind.) Sometimes, of course, when the temperature registers freezing, water changes from a liquid to a solid: ice or snow. But the water cycle is primarily a change from liquid to gas and back again.

A tremendous quantity of water goes through this cycle. Every year on our planet nearly 100,000 cubic miles of water evaporate into the air. (Try to picture how much water there is in just one cubic mile, a gigantic cube measuring one mile along each of its sides!) Since the quantity of water that evaporates is equalled by the amount that falls upon earth as rain and snow, it is this same great mass of water that returns to earth by condensation, some of it striking land where it soaks into the soil to provide moisture for plant life.

7

Cooling Effect of Evaporation

THE IDEA

Liquids require heat to evaporate. As heat is used up in this process, the place where the heat originally was is left cooler.

THE EXPERIMENT

Materials: A house thermometer, gauze or cotton, a rubber band, an eye dropper, and water.

Procedure:
1. Place a thermometer where wind will strike it and after twenty or thirty minutes, note the temperature.
2. Attach a little gauze or cotton to the bulb of the thermometer and dampen it with water. Again leave it in the wind for the same length of time and note the temperature.

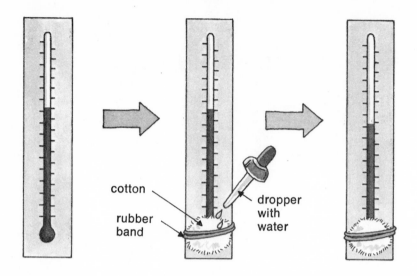

cotton

rubber
band

dropper
with
water

Conclusion: The temperature of the wet thermometer is several degrees lower than that of the dry one. This indicates that in the process of evaporation, energy in the form of heat is removed from the thermometer.

THE RELEVANCE

Where the climate is hot and dry, as in a desert, evaporating water cools water containers wrapped with wet burlap or some other wet material. As evaporation occurs, heat energy is absorbed from the containers and the water inside cools.

Nearly 600 calories of energy are absorbed for each gram

of water evaporated. You have certainly felt the effect of this process, especially when you have come out of the water after swimming. Your body feels cool even though the air temperature is high. And if the wind is blowing, the evaporation rate increases so much that you actually might feel cold enough to shiver.

8

Water Stores Heat

THE IDEA

Water stores heat more effectively than land does.

THE EXPERIMENT

Materials: Two metal cans the same size, water, soil, a kitchen oven, and a meat thermometer.

Procedure:
1. Fill the two cans to the same level, one with soil and one with water.
2. Place both cans in an oven set to "warm" and leave for two hours. If an oven is not available, place both cans in a place where they will be exposed to direct sunlight for several hours.
3. Remove the cans from the oven and place them somewhere

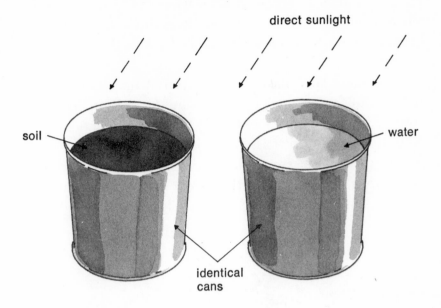

direct sunlight

soil

water

identical
cans

they can cool. From time to time, every hour or so, insert the thermometer in each and record the temperature.

Conclusion: You will find that the water retains its heat far longer than the soil does.

THE RELEVANCE

People who live near the seashore suffer less severe winters than those who live inland, for the heat stored in the ocean water warms the air over the shore. Farmers profit from this knowledge and, if they can, plant cold-sensitive crops near lakes where the air remains a few degrees warmer during the winter than in areas far from water. In central Florida, where it is important to prevent citrus crops from freezing, growers consider the most valuable land to lie between or among lakes.

Even major land masses, such as continents and countries, reflect water's warming effect. The Gulf Stream, an enormous river of water flowing clockwise in the North Atlantic Ocean, flows up our eastern coast and modifies the winter chill with water warmed in equatorial regions. As this tremendous ocean river circles the North Atlantic Ocean, it raises temperatures in Norway 20 to 25 degrees higher than one would

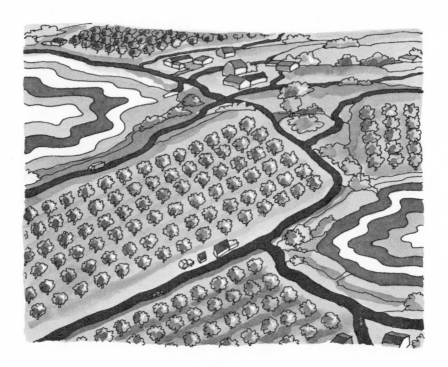

expect of this northern region. Because of the warmth of the Gulf Stream, the British Isles are far warmer than Labrador which is located in the same latitude but which receives no current of warm water. The southern coast of England is so warm that palm trees even grow there, a phenomenon that occurs only hundreds of miles farther south in continental Europe.

9

Water Pressure

THE IDEA

Water weighs over 62 pounds per cubic foot. Therefore, pressure increases greatly as a body of water increases in depth.

THE EXPERIMENTS

1

Materials: A large juice can, a sharp instrument to punch holes in the can, and water.

Procedure:
1. Punch four or five holes in the side of the can, more or less the same distance from one another, starting an inch from the top and finishing as close to the bottom as possible.
2. Over a sink, fill the can with water.
3. Observe the streams of water passing through the holes.

Conclusion: The closer the streams of water are to the bottom of the can, the stronger they are, indicating that water pressure increases with depth.

2

Materials: A small funnel of plastic or metal, rubber sheeting as from a balloon, plastic tape, about 3 feet of rubber tubing that will fit snugly over the tube end of the funnel, a piece of plastic or glass tubing of a size to fit the rubber tubing, water, and food coloring.

Procedure:

(Two people can assemble this apparatus better than one.)

1. Attach the rubber tube to the plastic or glass tubing. Bend it so that a large U is formed. Insert the small end of the funnel into the other end of the tubing. One leg of the U will be the plastic or glass tubing while the other leg will be the rubber tube with funnel.
2. Pour colored water into the funnel until it travels through the tubing and appears in the plastic or glass tubing. Continue to pour until it is about half full. Make certain that this leg of the U is never lower than the other or the colored water will spill.
3. Stretch the sheet rubber over the large end of the funnel and fasten securely with tape. Attach the small end of the funnel to the rubber tube.
4. Immerse the funnel in a bucket or any other large container of water and move the funnel in all depths and in such ways that the rubber sheeting is pointed in all directions.
5. Observe the relationship between the position of the fun-

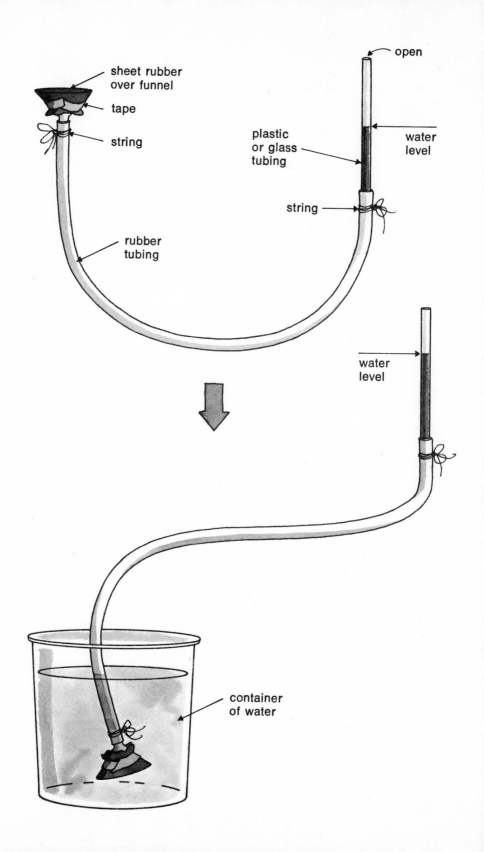

nel and the height of the colored liquid in the plastic or glass tubing.

Conclusion: The deeper you place the funnel in the water, the higher the liquid moves in the tubing, thus indicating that pressure increases with depth. How the rubber sheeting on the funnel is pointed has no effect upon the pressure, indicating that at any given depth the pressure is the same in all directions.

THE RELEVANCE

You have probably felt the effect of increasing water pressure on your body when you submerged deep in a pool or a lake. Most noticeable is the uncomfortable "pushing" feeling on the eardrums; this is relieved when you rise back to the water's surface.

Bathyscaphe *Trieste*

The column of water above an object that is at a depth of 33 feet weighs 15 pounds per square inch. That is, every square inch of your body or whatever is in the water at a depth of 33 feet has a pressure on it of 15 pounds. For every 33 feet deeper, another 15 pounds is added. The bathyscaphe *Trieste* submerged to over 35,000 feet in the ocean and was subjected to a pressure of over 14,000 pounds per square inch. Of course, devices designed to make deep ocean dives must have thick steel walls to withstand such pressures, or they would be crushed like an egg.

10

Buoyancy

THE IDEA

Water can support an object or cause it to float because of the lifting force it exerts on anything placed in it. This upward push increases as water becomes denser (see Chapter 1 on density).

THE EXPERIMENTS

1

Materials: A wide-mouth glass or plastic container, a ruler, oil-base modeling clay, a pencil, and paper.

Procedure:
1. Half fill the container with water. Place the ruler behind it, one end securely on the surface supporting the container, and record the water level.

2. Roll out a piece of clay until it is at least one-quarter inch thin. Fashion it into the shape of a bowl slightly smaller than the mouth of the container.
3. Carefully place the clay bowl right side up on the water so that it will float. With the ruler behind the container, again record the water level.
4. Carefully take the piece of clay out of the water and wad it up into a compact ball. Place it in the water and once again record the level the water rises to.

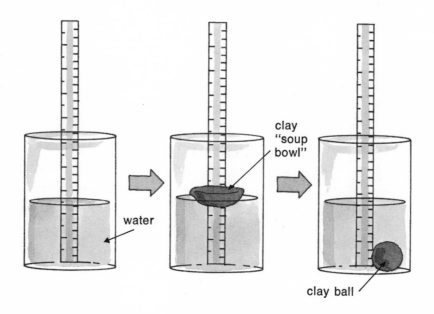

clay "soup bowl"

water

clay ball

Conclusion: The water level was higher when the clay floated than when it sank. This means that an object displaces more water when it floats than when it sinks. Therefore, the more water an object displaces the more buoyant it will be, or the more likely to float. When an object is spread over more water rather than less, its buoyancy increases because there is more water to "lift" it.

2

Materials: A spring balance, a kitchen scale, string, a 6- or 8-ounce fishing sinker, a container for water and a larger container to hold it, a piece of wood as large as will fit into the small container, water, a pencil, and paper.

Procedure:
1. Using a piece of string about 6 to 8 inches long, connect the fishing sinker and the spring balance as if you wished to weigh the lead.
2. Place the small container inside the larger one. Fill the smaller one with water to the top so that the least bit of rise in water level will cause an overflow into the larger container.
3. Note the weight of the fishing sinker on the spring balance. Lower the lead into the water and note what it now weighs.
4. Remove the lead from the water and, using the kitchen scale, weigh the amount that has overflowed. (First weigh it in the collecting container and then weigh the dry container alone. The smaller figure subtracted from the larger will give the weight of the water that has overflowed.)
5. Repeat step 2. This time attach the piece of wood rather than the fishing lead to the hanging scale and repeat the whole procedure.

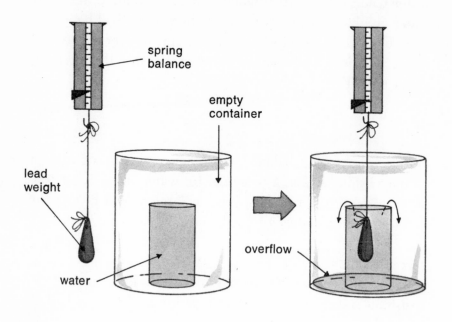

spring
balance

empty
container

lead
weight

overflow

water

Conclusion: The weight of water displaced by lowering the lead into it roughly equals the difference between the lead weighed in air and in water. At any rate, it is much less than the weight of the lead sinker. Also note that the weight of water the wood displaces is very nearly the same as the wood's weight in air. Therefore, an object will float if the water it displaces is equal to its own weight.

3

Materials: An egg, a container, water, and salt.

Procedure:

1. Place an egg in a container of tap water.
2. Carefully stir salt into the water until the egg floats.

Conclusion: Salt increases the density of the water. There-fore, the denser a liquid becomes, the more an object's buoy-ancy is increased.

THE RELEVANCE

If it were not for the tremendous amount of water displaced by a steel or concrete freighter, it would not float, for if solidly compacted, these materials would sink. Spreading their weight over a great surface area enables them to displace more water than if this were not the case, as illustrated in the experiment using clay. And because salt water is denser than fresh water and makes objects in it more buoyant, ships enter-ing the ocean from a lake or river actually float higher than they did in fresh water.

Displacement: Ocean-going tanker and yacht

11

Surface Film

THE IDEA

The surface of water is a tough film or skin which results from the tendency of water molecules to stick together. This attractive force is called cohesion.

THE EXPERIMENTS

1

Materials: A razor blade or sewing needle, a container of water, and soap or detergent powder.

Procedure:
1. Carefully place the razor blade or needle flat on the water so that when you remove your fingers, it floats. (Making the object only slightly oily will help.)
2. Once the razor blade or needle is floating, carefully scatter on the water surface soap or detergent powder.

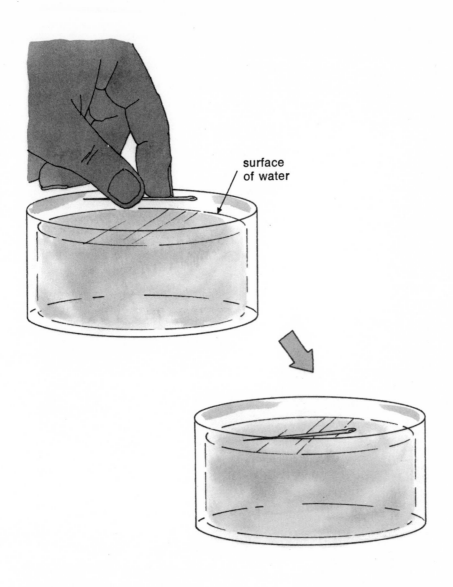

surface
of water

3. Observe what happens to the razor blade or the needle.

Conclusion: Razor blades and needles are made of steel which, being denser than water, should sink. But when the object is small enough and does not pierce the surface film that supports it, it floats. However, soap and detergent break up the surface film by destroying the cohesiveness of the water molecules, thus causing the object to sink.

2

Materials: Two small containers, water, and rubbing alcohol.

Procedure:

1. Fill the two containers to the same level, one with water and the other with alcohol.
2. After a few days note in which one there has been greater evaporation.

Conclusion: Alcohol evaporates more quickly than water as its molecules are less cohesive than water's.

THE RELEVANCE

The tough film on water enables certain insects to walk on its surface and not sink. Other animals, such as flatworms, cling to the underside of the film as they make their way through the water. This same surface skin surrounds a falling raindrop, making it tough enough to peck away at rocks and to gouge and displace earth. This is the reason a tiny object such as a raindrop has such a forceful impact upon solids and can, in time, reshape them completely.

12

Capillarity

Water defies gravity by rising in many different substances. This is because the attraction of water molecules for some materials (adhesion) is stronger than the attraction of water molecules for each other (cohesion).

THE EXPERIMENTS

1

Materials: Three or four open-ended glass tubes of different inside diameter (varying from a straw's diameter down to the diameter of the capillary tubes doctors and laboratory technicians use to collect blood from your finger), a 3 × 5-inch index card, clear tape, colored water, and a one- or two-cup glass or plastic container.

Procedure:
1. Half fill the container with colored water.

2. Tape the glass tubes to the index card. Then lower them into the colored water and keep them in an upright position.
3. Observe the level of colored water in the various tubes.

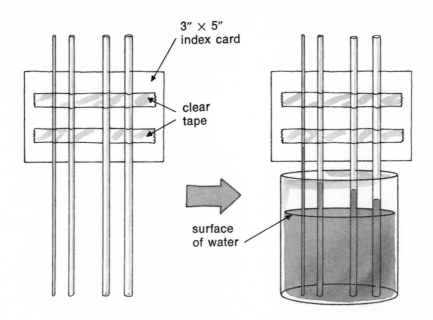

3" × 5" index card

clear tape

surface of water

Conclusion: Water rises the highest in the tubes of least diameter, demonstrating that the narrower the column of water, the less cohesion and the more adhesion it has.

2

Materials: Two microscope slides, colored water, and a shallow container such as a saucer.

Procedure:

1. Add food coloring to a little water in a small container until the color is quite distinct.
2. Squeeze together the two microscope slides and immerse only one corner in the colored water.
3. Observe how short a time it takes for the colored water to move by capillarity between the slides.

Conclusion: The thinness of the layer of water between the two slides results in great adhesiveness and little cohesiveness,

Giant Redwood

300 ft.

200 ft.

100 ft.

thus allowing the colored water to move rapidly, completely filling the space between the slides.

THE RELEVANCE

Because of capillarity and other forces, water rises in many materials such as a wick, a blotter, or cotton, and in plants. The narrowness of the water-conducting canals in plants is one factor enabling this to occur. When capillary action carries water to the top of giant redwood trees over 350 feet high, this phenomenon is truly remarkable.

13

Refraction of Light

THE IDEA

Water bends light rays as they pass through it, thus altering visibility.

THE EXPERIMENTS

1

Materials: A strong light source such as a powerful flashlight or a 200-watt clear bulb, a mask for the light made from black construction paper and cut so that only a pinpoint ray of light can pass through, a clear plastic or glass container, water, white paper, a pencil, a ruler, and a room that can be darkened.

Procedure:
1. Arrange the light source, mask, and container so that the ray of light will strike the container.

2. Place the paper under the container of water so that the light ray can be visually traced as it enters and exits the container of water. Darken the room. It is best to use the pencil and ruler and trace the path of light as it travels over the paper.

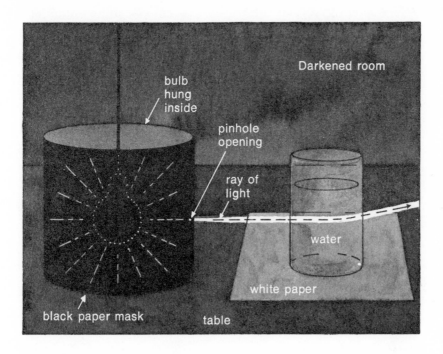

Conclusion: The light ray is bent as it passes through the water, demonstrating the phenomenon called refraction.

2

Materials: A shallow dish, a penny, and water.

Procedure:

1. Place the penny in the dish and lower your head so that the sides of the dish just conceal the penny from view.
2. Not moving your position, have someone pour water into the dish so as not to change the position of the penny.

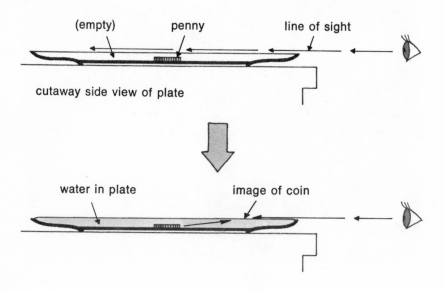

Conclusion: Once the penny is covered with water it comes into view, demonstrating that the water bends or refracts the rays of light from the penny to your eyes. The coin now seems placed in an entirely different position but, of course, it has not moved.

THE RELEVANCE

If you were to look at an angle through the surface of water at a submerged object, because of the way light rays from it are refracted or bent, you would see the object in a position where it really is not. To decide the real location of an object beneath the water's surface, one must understand how light is bent. This becomes very important when a fisherman wishes to cast a fly precisely where he thinks he sees a trout. Likewise, a person spearing fish must know that his target really is not where it appears to be.

BORIS ARNOV is Associate Professor of Education at Florida Atlantic University in Boca Raton, where he teaches methods of teaching science and English at elementary, secondary, and college levels to teachers. The winner of three National Science Foundation fellowships, he pursued his own graduate studies at Stanford University, the University of California at Berkeley, Bowdoin College, the University of Miami, and Chicago Medical School after graduating from Rollins College in Florida.

Professor Arnov has written eight previous books for young people, most of them on water-related subjects such as the deep sea, inland waters, and ocean ecology. Predictably, his favorite activities are fishing and boating.

GIULIO MAESTRO, a graduate of the Cooper Union Art School in New York City, is a versatile and well-known children's book illustrator. Many of the books he illustrates are written by his wife, Betsy. With their two small children, the Maestros live in Madison, Connecticut.